THE SHOW MUST GO ON

by

Mary Warren Foulk

Fernwood
PRESS

The Show Must Go On

©2025 by Mary Warren Foulk

Fernwood Press
Newberg, Oregon
www.fernwoodpress.com

All rights reserved. No part may be reproduced for any commercial purpose by any method without permission in writing from the copyright holder.

Printed in the United States of America

Cover and page design: Mareesa Fawver Moss
Cover art: Susan Allabashi at Billington Designs
Author photo: June E. Miller-Foulk

ISBN 978-1-59498-165-4

The "ending" Mary Foulk would wish for the "you," a beloved brother who died before he could embrace his life as a gay man, is the life she chronicles in this collection, addressing the loss of both parents as well as her brother while also exploring the nature of grief itself. She also chronicles the evolution of her own sexuality from the confusions of adolescence to coming out to marriage and parenthood with a beloved wife, but these poems do more than address essential themes; they soar off the page in a variety of forms—haiku, prose, erasure, anaphora—savoring language itself, poetry as song, in addition to honoring the challenges they address so articulately.

—Leslie Ullman
author of *Little Soul and the Selves* and *Library of Small Happiness*,
https://www.leslieullman.com/

The Show Must Go On is such a tender patchwork of sites. Sites of the queer horizons of sheets and midnight's kneeling. Sites of continual location and loss of the beloved brother. Of children begging for the uncle's story but having to settle for the silver frame his story dissolves in. Sites of gold sequins worn and of folds in a wallet. Of the tears staining the linen suit bought by a mother ten years ago. Of melba toast, scarves, bars, oceans, and eyes kept down. Ultimately this book is an invitation to witness what Foulk calls "the parentheses of living," conjured impressively with equal parts subtlety and heart-punch. Please read it.

—Carolyn Zaikowski
poet laureate of Easthampton, Massachusetts,
http://www.carolynzaikowski.com/.

This collection of emotionally electric poems is a reminder that our identities are constructed from our bodies and our stories. On a poetic tour of cemeteries, bedrooms, locker rooms, and bars, Mary Foulk orchestrates the uncomfortable truth that the source of our redemption is found in what we have been denied by ourselves and by others. Poetry reclaims what was lost.

—Michael Favala Goldman
poet/translator, author of *Small Sovereign* and *What Minimal Joy*,
https://michaelfavalagoldman.com/.

For Stephen, always

Contents

Not Just 9

I 11
   Confluence 12
   Lost Days 13
   My Father in Maine, 2013 15
   London Fog 16
   My Mother's Scarves 17
   Our Final Goodbyes 18
   Only fleeting images 19
   Self-Portrait with Erosion 20
   Lower Brandywine 22

II 23
   With Buck Teeth. With Braces. 24
   portrait of a queer as a young boy 26
   Urban Evening (2002) 27
   Remains 28
   Elegy with Black Suit 29
   The Show Must Go On 31
   Certainty 33

III 35
   If I Could Write You a Happier Ending 36

IV 43
   Corralling 44
   The Inventory of Fumbling 46
   It Is (She/She) 50
   Abomination in Sunlight 53
   Coming Out 54
   Wedding Invitation 55
   Wading 57

V 59
   Pink 60
   3 a.m. 61
   This Daily Reminder 62
   Answer 63
   If Obituaries Were Haiku 64
   When I Heard the Blessed Reverend 66
   One Afternoon 67
   Fragments 68
   Epilogue 69

Acknowledgments 71
Title Index 73
First Line Index 77

Not Just

              a box
              cedar urn
              with cross inlay
Not just surrounding dirt
              or white daisies
              sweeping the etched stone
Not just the cemetery
              of cracked headstones or
              a minister's attempt
              at preached comfort
Not just the limousine ride's
              medicated blur
              reception of tea sandwiches
              and ritual awkwardness
Not just one mourner
              one memory
Not just the obituary
              no one wanted to write
              about a life interrupted and
              adjectives that should
              have been uttered
Not just lawyers
              deconstructing
              your estate of found furniture
              and homoerotic art
Not just the funeral home's
              faint smell of ash
              and incomprehension
Not just that Sunday
              our Sundays

Not just assumptions   (not AIDS)
Not just our parents' disappointment—
          that closet that closet
Not just the silence
Not just religion's abominations   (count them)
          six biblical passages
Not just our childhood's red city
          red state
Not just Mother's antique trunk
          that holds what you last wore—
          that leather belt I bought you—
          those tortoise-shell glasses—
Not just the neighborhood boys
          you longed for
Not just your name

Confluence

Is it winter shadow
or darkening grief?
In this month
when anniversaries meet:
of birth and death, one
cannot relieve another
but rather sharpens the wound.
Vanilla cake and wrapped presents
reveal a vacant seat, a sorrow
no amount of singing
or prayer
or December days
can undo.

Lost Days

Those days when suspended by fear
they sat in near silence, perhaps a TV
in the background, a crossword on the table,

those days when they were daunted
by the doctor's diagnosis,
and we were daunted hearing their news,

days when we knew they were alone,
a blank refrigerator
and beds unmade,

when we were locked in our own timetables
and scheduled families, rushed holidays
and half-cheek kisses,

when we wished we'd asked more
questions about bloodlines and family histories,
about lost loves,

days when we recalled some distant memory
of their clapping wildly for our off-key notes
and failed trumpet explorations,

when they held our hands as we entered
new classrooms and mailed us long letters
to mend our homesickness

at sleepaway camp and later, college,
signed with hearts or a blur
of ink,

and then those days, like it or not,
when decisions were thrust upon us
without preparation,

long waiting hospital nights,
whispers, hoping
they could hear us,

days we prayed quietly or shouted,
grateful for any recognition,
a last hour or amen.

My Father in Maine, 2013

It is that twilight hour of orange sun
painting an August lake.
My father watches this familiar postcard
from a weathered raft close to shore,
as awed as I am observing him
in this dazzling, dimming light.
Outlined by the glare,
he is near skeletal,
bare skin covered loosely
by a sun-bleached bathing suit tied
with knotted string, impossible to untangle
for hands now incapable of stillness.
Once, his athletic swimmer's frame
carried me effortlessly to bed
despite my struggle against the evening's fatigue
and the thought of letting him go,
secure in the nestle of his woolen sweater
thin at the elbows with mixtured hints
of Old Spice and a cedar chest,
his soft voice lulling me into sleep
when ten uninterrupted hours,
a window's moon, and the safety
of cotton sheets promised
tomorrow.

London Fog

Searching your trench coat,

was I looking for truth? What I found instead,
a 1969 penny and a Green Room matchbook—

I resisted the flame.

Pockets, lined with moth holes
and a stained handkerchief,

not Mother's shade of red.

What can we ever know, Dad?
This urge to rummage our dead.

My Mother's Scarves

Like gallery paintings—
large geometric, bold black,
sequined silver—
collected through years of travel
and thrift store rummages.

Paris, Rome, a New York alley—
last-minute purchases, duty-free.
Scents of Aqua Net, mothballs,
regret.

I fold and unfold this inheritance, tracing seams
for her stories. The one I wear to her funeral,
cream-colored with gray flowers,
an understated square.

Our Final Goodbyes

Frail touch—an embrace
at the door, we linger
against the dwindling frame.

Slim bones shrouded
by a ragged sweater's
raw comfort, helpless
against what we know.

The months streaked
to gray, wrinkles and hair,
like wisteria

wilting

toward a whispered end.
"You're a good girl,"
thirty-six years' waiting,
this wince of words.

Only fleeting images

you can't grasp: auburn eyes, tanned skin,
a favorite lipstick—Revlon number six—
so delicately applied;

your thinking she will live forever, that
you can handle the news of a diagnosis too-soon
the chronic illness,
her crimson blood on sallow sheets;

when you consider the clinical hours
under surgical lights, stunned silences
between what and what not to say;

then, the inherited boxes
mildewing in the garage, costume jewelry
and tailored scarves, well-thumbed photographs
of sepia-toned family, nameless and choreographed,
frayed at the edges,

what you never knew, never thought to ask—
in your distracted state of childish wants,
chocolate milkshake, car keys,
ten dollars for a teenage date;

perhaps she heard
sweet music through the morphine drip,
saw angel wings and a radiant sun.
Perhaps she was filled with happiness—

somehow she knew you were on your way,
knew the plane was delayed,
knew you tried—God, you tried—

through the final breath.

Self-Portrait with Erosion

Do you remember
the sting of lemon sherbet
on our chins sunburnt
from hours playing
in white sand?

Riding bikes
bought at end-of-season
yard sales for $10 at best,
their squeaky wheels
and rusted shells?
Mine was red,
yours a pitch pine,
their pedals hummed
and clanged, making silhouettes
across tar.

Seagulls cried in the slow
breeze of ocean tides
eroding Stone Harbor.
And Grandmother's house
on 106th Street,
one of the last standing,
the only A-frame
with its pebble lawn
eclipsed by mini-mansions
on undersized lots.

Bare feet on the coarse
damp morning beach,
a long walk to the stone
boardwalk,
siblings breathing
in the shared air.

We watched fishermen
catch crabs
snapping against their
mortality.

Do you remember
the soft taffy
fresh from the loom
of an open window,
deep crowds waiting for
a sticky taste?

Later, with blistered skin,
we jumped sidewalk cracks,
hand in hand, on our meander
home.

Sea-air stained
bedsheets—
tattered curtains
flickering in salted windows—
background sounds of
crashing waves—
the ebb of our
childhoods' lullaby.

To visit now,
who am I
without you?

Lower Brandywine

At my brother's and parents'
graves, I wonder
about those who rest beside them.
Miss Sarah, "The Poet,"
to whom did she
write her final lines?

"World Travelers," Peg and Jim,
their rosy-hued seashells and rain-streaked
Polaroids—was it Paris and
Bombay?—resting askew at the borders
of their plot. And what about Stan,

"The Veteran," his rusted medals
and folded flags placed carefully
beneath his name?
His years, far fewer
than my own.

Do they share laughter
through the sediment,
grieve for the living?

Do they know that I visit
to lay daisies across their granite,
to offer prayers
from my restless hands?

Before I leave,
I trace the carved letters
of their names.

II

With Buck Teeth. With Braces.

after Chen Chen

With buck teeth. With braces. Without a night guard, which even now I refuse to wear in middle age, despite my dentist's plea. With my parents' glasses, oversized bottle lenses. With a Dorothy Hamill haircut. With clothing sewn by my mother in Lilly Pulitzer style. Without interest in Barbies or Lilly Pulitzer. With skinned knees and a desire to be the boy my father wanted. With my brother, who liked pink and listened to LPs of Cher. With red hair, freckles, sunburnt skin. With cutoffs I still fashion from old jeans. Without models but in hindsight perhaps the great-aunt who never married. With the girl from second grade, whose name I inked across posters scattering my room. With pink grapefruits, both sour and sweet, dusted lightly with sugar and traces of Palm Beach, where all good WASPs originate. With awkward shyness. With boys chasing girls. Without ever wanting to be chased by a boy. With silences at the dinner table. With my college roommate. With my mother's accusation of becoming a liberal at that school. With New York City. With my brother, navigating the East Village. With hide and seek. With girls' electric lips on the Clit Club dance floor. Without midnight remorse. With the morning's battle of shame and guilt. With coming out, going in, coming out, going in. With the towers falling. With darkness and burning smoke and it will happen again and mortality. With the searching. Without the knowing. With Sunday dinners at the 11th Street bar, my brother and I sharing stories of who we really were. With a tightening closet. With an anxious heart. Without him, trying to imagine a new world. With anger. With shattering. With fear and an honest letter to a broken family. With my partner in our Queens apartment. With the morning light draped across our mingled arms and legs. With the risk of feeling again. With a legal marriage. With a platinum band from Tiffany's, engraved like my grandmother's. With my father's champagne toast. With our children, placing ribboned bouquets on all their graves. With a vow to live the life my brother was denied.

portrait of a queer as a young boy

after Danez Smith

imagine a peacock, upon seeing other peafowl, hiding its gorgeous feather train, desirous for camouflage, perhaps even adoption by another related species, like common quail that blend into their natural surroundings, heard much more than seen. imagine rainbows seeking radiance beyond a raindrop. you don't like your young boy's reflection, scratch your face to make it new, pierce the skin for truth. see the scars of that clawing, the shedding of skin. behold what emerges, a seductive ocellus, so magnificent that eye of desire—boy sweet boy—love this worthy you.

Urban Evening (2002)

The world will end at 5:00 p.m.
Now, it's just five minutes to.

The young woman weaves
through a West Village crowd,
past men holding hands, past
the teenagers catcalling from a stoop.

She stops (at least a minute)
to pick tulips from a stranger's
sidewalk garden. She ruffles the ears
of a barking dachshund.

Her pace quickens as she nears
the corner bar where her brother
is waiting. Is she late, again?
His patience was always for her alone.

Another minute to cross the smoky
threshold, adjust to the dim.
The bartender motions hello and
points to where her brother had perched,

his cigarette still burning in the ashtray.
At first, she doesn't recognize the man
exiting the bathroom, the color fading
from this familiar face, how his hands tremble.

Now, the weight of his fall. A full minute
for 911, patrons scrambling. Another minute
to caress his hair. Against her whispering,
the final seconds tick, his name again and again.

Remains

Jimmy escorts us gingerly to a back room,
the electric hum another ache
as he turns on a glaring overhead and waits
for our eyes to adjust—

an affront of walnut paneling and
'70s mustard carpet. The walls have
an arm's-length smell
of mildewed decay.

Tiny shelves line the panels.
Their decorative patterns, geometric diagonals
of ceramic vases, like cookie jars
and empty wooden boxes.

There are well-marked sections.
Hello Kitty and Big Bird for children,
a brass eagle for the patriot or veteran.

We agree upon "Canterbury,"
the simplest rectangle, cherry-colored,
with a black-cross inlay. A tribute
to the writer, our brother.

Jimmy tells us it's a favorite
at the crematory. We anticipate
its finite contents, the sweet silt, charred bone,
the dust that remains.

Elegy with Black Suit

Time heals all wounds,
pronounced my great-aunt
upon hearing the news.
A centenarian, she had lived
through all the wars, even ones
of her own imaginings.
Each night,
she drank sherry and ate two
chocolates. She never married or
had children, which might explain
her fortitude and optimism.
She told dirty jokes, on repeat,
rendering visitors crimson and seeking
an exit. Because of her, I assumed
everyone aged.

He's in a better place,
from distant cousins and near strangers
while eating egg salad on Melba toast
and musing about the gathered:
who was the lover, despotic boss,
flirty colleague.
They recalled his brown eyes,
kind lilt of his voice. Kiss kiss,
hug hug, thank you for the tears
staining this suit,
linen, size 6,
bought by my mother ten years ago
(just in case), too tight in the waist.

At least he wasn't alone.
I held him as long as I could.
Just after, I walked
sunlit streets. The next day,
on the train, a man asked if he could sit
next to me. I cleared the seat
and nearly said aloud,
"You are beside the girl whose brother just died."
How many others are among us?

Get over it. Move on.
There was a yesterday, and
there is a today. The box
holds his ashes.
His fading laughter.
My mother's black suit,
our witness.

The Show Must Go On

I found this line
blurred on a faded Post-it, thin as a julep
mint, between folds
of your wallet, broken
at the leather seams.
A simple inheritance,
your lingering refrain.

The Show Must Go On,
a forgotten fragment
of our weighted legacy.
This spring twilight,
I have smelled the bourbon
crafted by a Virginia gentleman
in cut glass over ice crushed
and enveloped by young mint.

I have heard the echo of Mother's fraught
urging, the generations' monogram,
to "grasp the frosted pewter,"
you and I fallen branches
of the family tree, so bitter-
sweet the never-quite-fitting—

never-quite-able to play the part.
We found ourselves stateless, preferring
pinot, and there was your murmur.
The Show Must Go On,
this remembering, a selection,
omission.

Drunken laughter at our bequeathed dysfunctions,
those late Sunday afternoons at our East Village café.
Our sibling language,
like two debutantes drinking wistfully,
cigarette smoke curling around resonant words,
now a bourbon-less,

brother-less world.
What foretold your final curtain call?
How the streetlight framed your face,
your dimming stage lights,
one lasting reminder,
slurred
and bitter
as spearmint.

Certainty

Were his eyes near amber?
Was his favorite shirt
that peacock blue?

I can still feel the cold cotton
shrouded in plastic,
now stored in a steamer trunk
I visit once a year.

To remember,
to imagine anew
and again,
the fatal episode of his body folding,
the aftermath of numbing
questions.

To wonder,
was he real?
Was his
laughter—infectious?

To hold
the *what-ifs*
without answers,

fifteen years now,
twenty years
now.

III

If I Could Write You a Happier Ending

I.

we would be sitting on a porch in Maine,
the lake house of our imaginings from
those Sunday afternoons at the 11th Street bar,
Grandmother's antique rockers timed
to orange Sebago ripples,
toasts of chardonnay
to our mother,
who loved us as best she could,

sounds of our partners making dinner,
and in the background, hummed commentary
on our shared sibling language, our knowing
looks of queer childhood (survival),
my children begging for an uncle's story,
not the one dissolving in its silver frame

II.

the story would be alive in its silver frame,
you smiling for my camera,
the beautiful boy free
to be the right kind of boy,
to be the right kind of man,
a marching queen
shawled by rainbows
and a lover's tender hands,

gone the days of urgent cocks
in graffitied stalls, bar teases
of nameless numbers who never called—
a closet that swallowed you whole—
then cremation's fire, then mute dirt—heart attack
at forty

III.

your heart, just forty,
beginning to break
open to a lover's
moaned reassurance
of your worth, to graze
in the dimpled
light, map of your angles,
cartography of skin,
horizon of sheets

this horizon,
my squinting search,
any compass point
returns to
your death—my body
crawling toward that blue-black

IV.

crawling toward that blue-black,
it is morning, or it is night,
the planes did not strike,
our father dazzles
by Sebago's lake light,
our mother dances
to her shrine's
gentle men (gone)

these word temples
of love, your hand in
mine, mine in Alyson's,
Alyson's in our son's,
we walk again
together along the unknowable
horizon

V.

the horizon, unknowable,
yet your identity known,
no coming out, no regret,
no explanations
inked with shame and
midnight's kneeling, no streaked
guilt, no hiding in closets,

no need, no passing, travel without
fear, no tensed shoulders, dropping hands,
language unrecognizable, *my roommate*,
my friend, no either/or
alive/not
dead

VI.

not dead, alive,
we would have finished
our beers and the last drags of
cigarettes, waved goodbye
to Sierra, the bartender who
laughed at our Sunday reveries, then
wandered down St. Mark's in search of pasta
and other queers

that one I would fuck,
that one I would marry,
our little game, those evenings
under Manhattan streetlights,
our salvation of Sundays

IV

Corralling

I remember
running in circles,
August grass crunching
underfoot, our parents'
boozy bickering, and the suburban
neighbors barbecuing
too close to the fence.

"Faster," he said.

I was seven, maybe eight,
following his command—
anything for his praise.

The summer had been too long,
too lonely without him.

"Faster," he said.

Raised to be a (tom)boy by our father,
a Southern debutante by our mother,
I drifted tensely in-between.

My legs were strong.

"Don't look. Keep running."

What had he learned
at that overnight camp?
The one that took him so
far away, eight weeks,
an eternity.

"Get ready."

For what?

Legs—breath—attention—please ...
legs—breath—attention—please ...
the slow whistle
of the lasso.

My bare feet skimmed
the brittle surface,
then slightest burn
of rope tracing shoulders, arms,
legs. Ankles jarred together,
locked midair.

An unforgiving lawn.
I lay coiled,
breathless.

Now, corralled.
The girl in the white dress
with bleeding knees.

The Inventory of Fumbling

after Carmen Maria Machado

Two girls and a boy, seventh grade.
I scribble your names next to small hearts and sparkly rainbows, on posters of teen idols and kittens, centerfolds taken from cheap magazines targeting 10- to 14-year-olds with their own awakenings to lust. I stare at their angles from a twin bed by the drafty window with sunflower curtains. At night, I add more hearts, a feverish red, and singsong your names quietly, like a sultry lullaby, behind a closed door. I want to kiss and hug you, so unsure of the new flutterings, my searching fingertips. I like the feel of your smiles each day at school, the slight touch of your hair when I sit behind you in class, your smell like fabric softener, chocolate, fresh-cut grass. I plaster your names like wallpaper that Mother redecorates one morning after the school bus departs.

The locker room, high school.
It's best to keep my eyes down. Which is hard to do, after practice, in the showers with other young girls like me, growing into their own curves and breasts and pubes, their arms and legs taut from training, their skin golden from hours under a spring sun. This team, the daily practice, the wins and losses, our familial embrace. And the captain, my god, like a gazelle, so unaware of her own prowess, her own agile beauty. It is confusing to want more from the quick hug before play. Confusing to feel another's gaze along my body, as I wash away the day, as I slowly dress and undress.

The dorm boyfriend, college.

Is it sex if I can't remember it? The midnight beer and pawing and cracks of morning light. The search for soiled clothing. Scrambled eggs and burnt toast. Maybe a final kiss, some hungover tongue before goodbyes. Each weekend on repeat. It's what I was taught. It's what I felt I had to do. He doesn't notice when I spend more and more time with my roommate. I am his. Even as she fills my mind, as the boyfriend pounds away, as I orgasm to the prayer-like mouthing of her name.

That girl, graduate school.
The child psychology professor says, "Pick a partner," and our eyes meet. After class, she asks me to go dancing. That night, I pick her up at her apartment in Spanish Harlem; she is wearing gold sequins and nothing else. I freeze while she whispers in my ear, "I like you." I suggest a back rub and watch as she goes places I never thought possible. In the morning, we feel the sun traipse across our tangled bodies and then write poems while eating cereal. Mine is about cartography and exploring new worlds. Hers, like e.e. cummings, about the taste of wild blueberries coated in Maine dew.

It Is (She/She)

they don't want to stop
they can't stop
they've been going at it for days now
for months years
she's on top of her
she's on top of her
the lingering between legs
fingers in mouth
grazing teeth
teasing tongues
it is spring
it is fall
grass green
and lush and
burnt-orange leaves
tumble to earth
falling to a certain death
mixing with dirt and seed and souls
reborn again and again
it is she always
it is March-April
that tension
between
ice chill and
cherry blossom
the lost hour
between forward and back
it is July
and she is reeling in
torrents of heat
nipple brushes
fingers search
and twine

eyelids flutter
teardrops
there is a whispered whimper
there is a hallelujah song
it is twilight
it is noon
she and
she
enveloped in
sheets of rain
moist
mirrored
entering
entering
what is truth?
bills and
groceries and
dirty dishes piled
in a rusted sink
dripping
bathtub
overflow of
warm water
cascading
over edges
so many edges
and curves
kneecap elbow
mountain valley
hers
it is silver dust
and scarlet sage
and soft soft

tonality
it is
perhaps
even
a kind of deity
Shiva
Buddha
Christ
this worship, this
what she longs for
what she'll never
quite have
the gaps
September crevices
it is never enough
will never be enough
on top
on bottom
from behind
what is
enough?
a black iris
redemption
a plunging of self
fervently
into the
deep
deep
well

Abomination in Sunlight

We wander slowly
down a sunlit Chelsea street,
lingering in maple casts
across aging brownstones.

I hold Alyson's hand,
our fingers intertwining
with the graze of silver bands.

A young man
walks toward us,
his strange approach
near neighborly.

As he ignores our nod,
we tense quickly,
his path now clear.

Against his eyes,
against his jarring break,
this tenuous hold,
we steel,
our joy.

His fleeting "abomination,"
his laughing
into an urban crowd.

My mother's warning,
you will be less.

And red tulips on doorsteps
alert us to this
cloudless afternoon.

Coming Out

I
I came
I came out
I came out again
I came out again again

        Hello, I am...............

        Hello, I

        Hello,

        Hello

        Am I?

        Am I

        Am

        I

again again out came I
again out came I
out came I
came I
I

Wedding Invitation

Come out, and look, you daughters of Zion. Look on King Solomon wearing a crown, the crown with which his mother crowned him on the day of his wedding, the day his heart rejoiced.
—From Song of Solomon 3:11

Mr.
heterosexual not *gay* gender-conforming male [using pronouns he, him]
and
Mrs.
heterosexual not *lesbian* gender-conforming female [using pronouns she, her]
Levi Gomorrah
request the privilege of your *natural* not unnatural presence at the federal- and state-sanctioned *marriage* not domestic partnership not civil union not of their *heterosexual* not *lesbian* gender-conforming female [using pronouns she, her] daughter
Ms. Ruth
to
Mr. Timothy
heterosexual not *gay* gender-conforming male [using pronouns he, him] son
of
heterosexual not *gay* gender-conforming male [using pronouns he, him] **Captain**
and
heterosexual not *lesbian* gender-conforming female [using pronouns she, her] **Mrs.**
Paul Romans

Saturday, the Twenty-Fifth of August
Two Thousand Fourteen
Four o'clock p.m.
THE CHURCH
where
ALL ARE WELCOME

Except
Abominations and Sodomites

If those Deadly Sinners must attend,
please seat them in the last pew
by the balcony's serpentine staircase
and at the reception
by the checkbox parquet dance floor
with all the other tattooed bicoastal Queers drinking cosmos,
the thrice-divorced cousins seeking new spouses, and
chain-smoking Great Aunt Margaret
who recently transitioned
and blows kisses
to the anthemic salvation,
"I Will Survive"

Wading

Wading in each other's shadows, this night,
we endure. Murky air and bedroom fog,
the demon arguments have returned. Bills
past due, the day's logistics, loss of lust.
Not so subtle shifts in solemn, sobering
corners. Echo somber sheets, cold rustlings,
her muted breath. Despite feigned attempts
at sleep, there is no room for dreaming. Thread-
bare fantasies no longer guide. Will
she remember our first date? That cloudless
sky and urban meadow, a festival
of chanting monks in saffron bliss. Later,
the gentle wind sang carnal haiku. Five-
seven-five. We came so easily. The
slightest touch, a slow undoing.

Exhale the slow undoing, slightest touch.
Her lips on my breast, nipple in mouth.
We merge, again and again,
this twined mingling. Tracing
the cracks in our white mortar. Foundation
still holding, still holds. Our most gradual
gathering of grayed black-and-whites, book-lined
shelves, and torn calendars marking blue/pink birth,
unsettled death. Moonlit patterns etched
deeply across these bodies and walls. Breath, buoyed
by memory and callused fingertips,
ready the move from wading.
Feel me, love, in this night,
in our shadows.

V

Pink

after Mary Ruefle

Pink sadness is Adam's rib swathed in an apron, still reeling from the ring of fire. Pink is that beautiful sadness of birth wrapped in pink cotton blankets. Pink sadness is the yawns of newborns and husbands napping unaware of sour laundry or antique dishes crusting in the sink. It is the sadness of scented vows, lost in the back of a dresser drawer, sometimes found on a random Sunday or reread at milestone cocktail parties. Pink sadness is the snapshot sunsets and sunrises witnessed during daily commutes and the ticked hours between strong coffee and evening's last kiss. Pink sadness is soft lips on a child's sleeping cheek. It is the mantel memory of mothers and grandmothers, their imperfect models smiling back. Pink sadness is the daughters they create.

3 a.m.

Did I hear the doors lock,
the cold metal sync?
Did I draw the curtains,
thwart the neighbor's watchful
eye? Did I turn off the stove,
align the knobs to
Off Off Off?
Did I feed the cats, both
the one staring at me
with her hazel eyes
and the one nestled next to you,
keeping time with your snoring,
her purr a heavy rasp,
a dying elder we rescued,
namely to rescue us?
Did I tell you I love you,
even say goodnight?
Did I listen for the children's
breath, lean my face next to theirs
to stare at their
dreaming and wonder why they don't hear
these questions and other noises—
the lone owl singing
atop the swaying pines?
Did I add to tomorrow's lists
what already I have forgotten—
tasks taped to the bathroom
mirror, torn and
streaking? Will it ever be dawn,
and will I ever
be enough?

This Daily Reminder

My children chase each other
in the spring garden,
their hands grasping at air.
My son pauses to gather
daffodils with bright stems,
then arranges them in bunches tied
with string to clasp
around his younger sister's
neck like jewels—

yellow, like the ones
in our grandparents' backyard
near the cemetery of broken headstones
that haunted our dreams,
flowers you tucked behind my ears
while my six-year-old hands fidgeted
and made you mad, yet I could see you
smile through the camera—
you were fourteen, and I adored
you even when
the sun was setting and I was hungry.

I can see it all
in that photo as I see it
this afternoon in my daughter—
later, we will place the flowers
as centerpieces at the table
where we leave your
empty chair.

Answer

I swear I heard
one recent morning,
riding across Hawthorne Bridge—
was it shifting firs?
Willamette waves? The ripples
echoed memories of our parents'
slow summer splintering,
our bedtime stories, their arguments,
our whispers under fortress sheets,
a makeshift tent where I could lean
into you and prop my head against
your pillowed shoulder as we ignored
their calls for goodnight.
Today, I'm the restless mother watching
the clock as my youngest struggles
with her favorite sneakers, the ones
with flowers and mud streaks, the ones
that make her feel like speed itself,
capable of flying and climbing trees.
I wonder at her grace as she wings
through branches, my ready hands—
like yours—
a net to catch her fall.

If Obituaries Were Haiku

("Obituaries." *The News Journal*,
Every Month, Every Year.
Accessed June 11, 2002.)

Here lies a lover,
rider of bathtub oceans,
carousel ponies.

*

Our Heroine has
fallen—the movie ended.
Sunsets are fragile.

*

Dried, hanging roses.
Winter cabernets. Remnants
linger, like dust, love.

*

His smiling ghost speaks
of sibling rivalries, their
magic carpet rides.

*

"She lived as she died."
Summer's sequin fantasy,
bar stool, whiskey lust.

*

The Inheritance—
Father's blue-green eyes, Aunt Ruth's
Ethel Merman tapes.

*

Measures of a life—
red marrow, cum, hint of ash—
framed photographs, stains.

When I Heard the Blessed Reverend

When I heard the blessed reverend,
the biblical saints catalogued at length,
when I reread the passages of my religious education,
the Book of Micah, the Book of Ruth,
faint recall of their meanings,
when I, sitting, heard the reverend where he lectured
with called hallelujahs and whispered amens
in time to the sanctuary's grieving,
how soon I became lost in the murmuring words,
this sacred din, till rising from my white processional chair,
I touched the wooden urn before me,
urgent for my brother's dust,
a stained glass
infinite.

One Afternoon

Sitting on your king-size bed. Grandfather's four poster with cabriole legs. (A grandfather we never knew.) Scratch of a handmade quilt, woven blues and golds, slightly moth-eaten at the edges. Was it May? Late summer? Stripes of afternoon sun through a screened window. We were listening to your albums. Elton John or maybe some musical you were obsessing over. Stick of our skinned knees. Cross-legged and distracted. A vinyl's skip. You taught me how to place the turntable needle, careful steadiness of your hands, vulnerability of the grooves. "Benny, Benny, Benny and the Jets." Lost in your company one afternoon. A heartbeat some forty years later on this five-state drive to plant lilies by your name.

Fragments

their fragments
wake me
in the dark

to fumble
still coated
by the scattered
ashes

lines
already written
host of guides

help me
forge
my words
breath

pieces from
a vase
shattered

remnants
of clay, memory
moment
and want

a space
of desire
basic, urgent
made

Epilogue

Prune the blades
around the edges.
Pull the dandelions
at the root.

If there is time,
blow florets
in the breeze.

Brush the stone
of mud and dead grasses.
Trace the grooves—
each name pray aloud.

Remember, again,
their parentheses of living,
how you loved
between the immovable dates.

When you rise to leave,
kiss the concrete slowly,
slowly

with your fingertips,
note the cold earth
under your nails.

Acknowledgments

I offer grateful acknowledgment to the editors of the following publications in which poems from this collection first appeared:

"Answer," "Certainty," "Epilogue," and "Fragments" from the chapbook *If I Could Write You a Happier Ending*, Dancing Girl Press, 2021. Copyright © Mary Warren Foulk.

Arlington Literary Journal (Gival Press), "Abomination in Sunlight," "My Mother's Scarves," "The Inventory of Fumbling."

Cathexis Northwest Press, "Elegy with Black Suit," "The Show Must Go On," "Wading."

Derailleur Press, *The Rail*, "My Father in Maine, 2013."

Evening Street Press, "Urban Evening (2002)."

Inanna Publications, *(M)othering: an anthology*, "3 a.m."

Los Angeles Poet Society, "Coming Out," "Wedding Invitation."

Lucky Jefferson, "Confluence."

My Loves: A Digital Anthology of Queer Love Poems (Ghost City Press), "With Buck Teeth. With Braces."

Palette Poetry, "If I Could Write You a Happier Ending."

River Heron Review, "portrait of a queer as a young boy."
Sheila-Na-Gig, "Self-Portrait with Erosion."
The Hollins Critic, "If Obituaries Were Haiku."
The Ignatian Literary Magazine, "Not Just."
The Midwest Quarterly, "Our Final Goodbyes."
Visitant, "London Fog."
VoiceCatcher, "It Is…(She/She)."
Waterwheel Review, "Corralling."
Yes, Poetry, "Pink."

I offer my love and gratitude to my wife, children, and extended family for their steadfast belief in me. Many helped shape this collection. My deepest appreciation to Vermont College of Fine Arts advisors Leslie Ullman, Betsy Sholl, Parneshia Jones, and Kathleen Graber for their transformative teaching and compassionate guidance; and to my VCFA cohort for their ongoing encouragement and generous kindness. To my inspiring mentors at Pioneer Valley Writers Workshop and Straw Dog Writers Guild: Kate Senecal, Carolyn Zaikowski, Joy Baglio, Gail Thomas, Caroline Belle Stewart, Michael Favala Goldman, and Liz Bedell. To my close friends and invaluable editors—Pascale Giroux, Sarah Levine, Siarra Riehl, Jan Freeman, and Susan Allabashi, who designed the stunning cover. Lastly, my profound thanks to Fernwood Press and to Eric Muhr for their remarkable support and celebration of my work—and to magical poet Annie Lighthart for leading me there. I am honored that *The Show Must Go On* found this extraordinary home.

Title Index

Numbers
3 a.m. 61

A
Abomination in Sunlight 53
Answer 63

C
Certainty 33
Coming Out 54
Confluence 12
Corralling 44

E
Elegy with Black Suit 29
Epilogue 69

F
Fragments 68

I

If I Could Write You a Happier Ending 36
If Obituaries Were Haiku 64
It Is (She/She) 50

L

London Fog 16
Lost Days 13
Lower Brandywine 22

M

My Father in Maine, 2013 15
My Mother's Scarves 17

N

Not Just 9

O

One Afternoon 67
Only fleeting images 19
Our Final Goodbyes 18

P

Pink 60
portrait of a queer as a young boy 26

R

Remains 28

S

Self-Portrait with Erosion 20

T

The Inventory of Fumbling 46
The Show Must Go On 31
This Daily Reminder 62

U
    Urban Evening (2002) 27

W
    Wading 57
    Wedding Invitation 55
    When I Heard the Blessed Reverend 66
    With Buck Teeth. With Braces. 24

First Line Index

A

a box 9
At my brother's and parents' 22

D

Did I hear the doors lock 61
Do you remember 20

F

Frail touch—an embrace 18

H

Here lies a lover 64
heterosexual not *gay* gender-conforming male 55

I

I 54
I found this line 31
imagine a peacock, upon seeing
    other peafowl, hiding its 26
I remember 44

Is it winter shadow 12
I swear I heard 63
It is that twilight hour of orange sun 15

J

Jimmy escorts us gingerly to a back room 28

L

Like gallery paintings 17

M

My children chase each other 62

P

Pink sadness is Adam's rib swathed
   in an apron, still 60
Prune the blades 69

S

Searching your trench coat 16
Sitting on your king-size bed.
   Grandfather's four poster 67

T

their fragments 68
The world will end at 5:00 p.m. 27
they don't want to stop 50
Those days when suspended by fear 13
Time heals all wounds 29
Two girls and a boy, seventh grade 46

W

Wading in each other's shadows, this night 57
Were his eyes near amber? 33
We wander slowly 53
we would be sitting on a porch in Maine 36
When I heard the blessed reverend 66

With buck teeth. With braces.
   Without a night guard, which 24

Y
   you can't grasp: auburn eyes, tanned skin 19

www.ingramcontent.com/pod-product-compliance
Lightning Source LLC
Chambersburg PA
CBHW010047090426
42735CB00020B/3417